ME

A[ ]   ONE

D1462915

MEDITATION
FOR
ABSOLUTELY EVERYONE

A Complete Guide

by Subagh Singh Khalsa

CHARLES E. TUTTLE CO., INC.
BOSTON • RUTLAND, VERMONT • TOKYO

Published by Charles E. Tuttle Co., Inc. of Rutland, Vermont
and Tokyo, Japan with editorial offices at 153 Milk Street,
5th floor, Boston, MA 02109

Library of Congress Cataloging–in–Publication Data
Khalsa, Subagh Singh.
        Meditation for absolutely everyone : a complete guide/
by Subagh Singh Khalsa.
        p.   cm.
    ISBN 0-8048-3011-8
    1. Meditation.   I. Title.
BF637.M4K48   1994
158'.12--dc20

                                    9-6862
                                    CIP

    5 7 9 10 8 6

Printed in Singapore

🍂 CONTENTS 🍂

A NOTE TO THE READER

To get the most out of this book and tape, read through the book before you begin to use the tape. As you read the section describing each different meditation, take note of the ones to which you are most attracted. Then, to begin your own meditation practice, reread the instructions for the mediation with which you want to begin, find that meditation on the tape, and begin your practice. If you are not drawn to any particular meditation, do them all in the order presented, starting with the deep relaxation.

It would be wise to begin by making a commitment to yourself to practicing at least one meditation a day, every day for six weeks. For most people, the best times to practice are in the early morning or in the evening before bed.

🍃 INTRODUCTION 🍃

This book and tape will give you the experience of meditation. You want peace and happiness in life. You could probably also benefit from less tension, better health, more energy, clearer thought, less emotionalism, more loving relationships, and better concentration. All these benefits can come to you if you meditate. Meditation can improve athletic performance, grades in school, and efficiency at work. More importantly, few of us can progress very far spiritually without some form of regular meditation.

Meditation can serve you at many levels, whether you are facing serious illness, have a goal of avoiding stress and relieving tension, wish for personal growth, or desire spiritual liberation. It can help you with specific goals such as improving your golf game. It can help with more general goals such as gaining financial success or becoming more peaceful. Meditation owes its tremendous versatility to the fact that human achievement comes easiest to those capable of concentration, relaxation, and clarity of thought. You can develop these three qualities by meditating.

You may choose to focus your concentration on God, on your breath, on achieving business objectives, or on getting a little white golf ball to drop into a hole. Whatever your goals, improved powers of concentration will serve you.

Tension at work, chronic pain, high blood pressure, or nervousness about a date with someone you feel attracted to can all be reduced with the relaxation that meditation will give you.

Clarity of thought will serve you whether you need to take an exam, develop a success strategy, or get past the emotions sabotaging a relationship.

Create your own goals. Determine the uses to which you put the skills developed in meditation. But in any case, rest assured that the regular practice of meditation will enhance your life.

We exist in an environment that may or may not be all we wish for. Some of us hope to advance ourselves, to rise above whatever limits our environment or our minds seem to impose. If you see yourself as such a person, as one who desires personal growth, you have to make the first move yourself. Don't expect it to come from other people or from the world around you. The stress of your job, the disabilities you must live with, or the imperfections of your relationships will not stop of their own accord. They will certainly not stop just because you wish them to. But you can stop yourself. You can stop the inner battles.

Beyond your stress resides a peace. You can

put yourself into that peace and expect nothing from the outside. You can learn to accept, without fear or retreat, whatever your situation presents you with. When you learn to do that, you will find that every situation contains opportunity and that you will be able to make use of it.

We all have a higher nature, whether or not we are aware of it. Anyone with a mind, with consciousness, can become awakened to that higher nature. You may feel bad about the activities of your lower self. You may not accept your pride or your selfishness or your ill health. You can probably identify problems you ought to solve. Start your meditative practice by accepting these "problems" as good things. They are, after all, the very motivation for meditation. Gather up all these "negative" things, just as a gardener might gather up manure, dead leaves, or kitchen scraps. Don't try to throw them away; acknowledge and accept them. Use them. Let them become the compost. Let them become wonderful new soil in which your better consciousness can grow. If you were to try to throw out the negative then part of who you have been up until now would have been wasted. Carefully study your pain. Examine your fears. Look directly at the negative side of your self-image. Go through the pain of it so that you may obtain a deeper self-knowledge.

At the same time, examine your positive side and all you have done that you feel good about. Gather this up as well, and add it to your self-knowledge. Go into all of it in depth. Develop a panoramic awareness, accepting it all, fully accepting yourself at this moment.

I am not talking here of some mystical experience or anything mysterious—just a peaceful awareness of what exists now. This requires not allowing memories of the past or expectations of the future to influence you. You will find that you can let down your barriers this way. No matter how great the conflicts or issues in your life might seem, you can accept them all with patience.

Of course this is easier if you find yourself in a quiet spot on a sunny day; but this is often not possible. You may be surrounded by the wrong people, or feel angry or depressed, or live on a noisy street. And, even if everything does appear to be quite favorable, you will not easily escape from all the emotional disturbances in your mind. Face it all with acceptance and quiet patience. This is the first step in producing peace.

As many people begin to meditate, they become frustrated because their minds won't stay still. Hundreds of unconnected and unwanted thoughts disturb their meditation. Don't worry about that. Instead, accept all these thoughts in the very same way that you must accept your pain, your external environment, or your emotions.

When thoughts come along, just watch them. Don't try to suppress them. Thoughts have a very vaporous nature. They have no real substance. When they come into your mind observe them without any attachment and without any rejection. Just return to meditation. Don't think of this as a struggle. Make no attempt to control yourself or not control yourself, or even to feel peaceful. Just meditate.

Don't seek something when you meditate. What comes to you when you meditate could be called knowing as opposed to knowledge, being as opposed to becoming, or perhaps awareness as opposed to opinion. Let go of "I" as in: "I wish to achieve." Don't think at all about the future or right or wrong. Forget striving and reward. Meditate without purpose, expectation, or judgment.

Many people reject the possibility of meditation because they believe they just can't sit still or that they have too much nervousness to relax. People like that can usually do surprisingly well with meditation if they just begin with very brief sessions. Later they extend their practice periods a little, soon learning that their nervousness represents a learned coping mechanism (albeit an ineffective one) and not some inborn trait. As their practice continues, their habit of nervousness slowly drops away, replaced by more useful traits such as calmness and relaxation.

Everyone can meditate and everyone can reap its benefits. I have enjoyed meditating with very young children, 85-year-olds, clergy of many different faiths, competitive athletes, corporate executives, and people on welfare. I have meditated with the sick and dying as well as with those in vibrant good health. I have meditated with retarded people, and I have meditated with those who have serious addictions, chronic mental health problems, and histories of abuse. I have meditated alone and in groups of over one thousand people.

You too can meditate and benefit from the practice. I can think of only two absolute prerequisites. First, you must have consciousness. Believe me—you qualify. Second, you have to be willing to practice. You can't take meditation as you might take a pill. Bringing yourself to a meditative state requires some discipline. You will not benefit much if you just sit and listen to the tape included with this book once or twice. You must participate. Set aside your doubts, ignore any distractions, and allow yourself to have the experience of meditation. Nothing I write can substitute for that experience.

You have within you the power to create further personal growth, greater health and success, and deeper happiness in your own life. Your job can give you real joy. Your relationships don't have to hurt. You can heal emotional pain. You can handle, without undue tension, the greatest challenges in your life. And you can achieve (with greater ease than you ever believed possible) any realistic goals you set for yourself.

I invite you now to do something that will quite possibly result in the most positive, healing changes of your entire life. Picture yourself more calm and relaxed, more centered, more effective. Feel what it would be like to concentrate better. Hear your own voice expressing clarity of thought. Sense what it would be like to rise above pain or negative emotions. Meditation could do all of this for you, and more. Meditate. Invest in yourself. And enjoy.

1

🍃 AN OVERVIEW
OF MEDITATION 🍃

Meditation penetrates right to the very source of our happiness. It liberates us from the notion that feeling good or bad results from what happens to us. It replaces that false notion with the understanding that our attitude towards life counts for much, much more.

Attitude determines happiness as well as suffering. Direct your efforts at your attitude, and both happiness and peace of mind will come to you. The promise of meditation boils down to this: you have the power to create peace of mind and happiness no matter what may happen to you.

Do you find yourself angry when wronged, distraught over an illness or a loss, or greedily attached to the things you want? Emotions like these, and not the events that "cause" them, lead to the pain and suffering in life. We truly have the ability to transcend this suffering and to find happiness regardless of our circumstances.

> *"We who lived in concentration camps can remember the men who walked through the huts comforting others, giving away their last piece of bread. They may have been few in number, but they offer sufficient proof that everything can be taken from a man but one thing: the last of the human freedoms—to choose one's attitude in any given set of circumstances, to choose one's own way."*

> Viktor Frankel

Meditation gives the power to make that choice. Meditation frees the mind from its constant moving and restlessness. It allows you to develop calmness and insight. By meditating you can see deeper into the reality of your own existence and experience yourself with exquisite sensitivity. With meditation you continue along your path of self-discovery, discarding obsolete emotional patterns and developing new vision.

POSITIVE MIND–NEGATIVE MIND –NEUTRAL MIND

By what power does meditation achieve all this? When you meditate you develop what is called the neutral mind. This neutral mind is distinguished from the positive or the negative minds which you naturally possess from birth. Imagine a tiny infant hungry or startled. She does not yet have a neutral mind. Her negative mind (and an instant later her lungs) sends out its clear message: "I don't like this. Fix it now!" Later, soothed and cuddled and fed, the baby's positive mind sends out entirely different messages and we get smiles and sweet baby sounds that melt our hearts.

The positive mind tells you what good might come out of a situation. It represents your optimistic side and your ability to have and give hope. People with an underdeveloped positive mind tend towards negativity, depression, and feelings of hopelessness.

The negative mind at its most useful warns of danger and helps you calculate the possible pitfalls in any situation. Those with too little of this capacity may, for example, rush blindly into relationships that ultimately hurt. But with too much of a negative mind, they may always criticize, hold back, or relate to their fears.

Both minds serve in their own way, each balancing the other. The ideal balance is the neutral or meditative mind. It represents the ability to understand what course of action will serve best, what attitude gives the greatest happiness, and even which people are the best to associate with.

A neutral mind does not come naturally. You have to develop neutrality just as you would develop any other skill. An athlete practices her sport, a musician practices his instrument, and those who long for peace of mind practice meditation and related techniques to learn neutrality.

DUALITY

Most of the difficulty we have in achieving durable happiness results from duality, the opposite of neutrality. This mental state develops because our positive and negative minds ceaselessly judge and categorize. We call some things good and others bad. We call some people friends and others enemies.

We do not make all of these judgments according to objective criteria. They emerge out of our own subjective standards. Our self-centered nature, operating through our positive and negative minds, creates this duality. It has no existence, no reality, of its own. Endless energy (both mental and physical) then goes into avoiding those parts of our world that we don't like and seeking out those parts that we do. On the one hand we have desire. On the other hand fear. Neither permits us peace of mind.

Imagine the advantage of understanding the world with neutral minds. All experiences would appear equally rich in meaning. A migrant farm worker would receive the same respect as a surgeon. Storms would become as delightful as sunshine. Duality robs us of all the peace and joy of neutrality.

NEUTRALITY

In becoming neutral, you will not give up your preferences. You may still have a strong preference for a job with less stress, that pays more and uses your skills better. But with neutrality your mind doesn't have to be dominated by frustration with your present job or with a burning desire for something better. You will more easily accept what you have—even while you develop clarity about what a better job might offer, and make effective use of your energy to train for and find that perfect job.

The neutral mind will free you from the grip of negative emotionalism. Lust, anger, greed, pride, and attachment gradually will give way to love, forgiveness, generosity, humility, and acceptance. Joy will replace fear. Sadness, insecurity, and guilt will lose their power. Whereas the emotional roller coaster drains you, neutrality will leave you with energy, enthusiasm, and passion to accomplish what you care about. When you fail, when life knocks you down, when tragedy strikes, neutrality will help you to accept that. In disappointing or trying times, neutrality will allow healing and give you the capacity to pick yourself up and try again.

In neutrality you will drop the erroneous sense of yourself as a victim. The things that happen to you will lose their power over your state of mind. In each event, no matter how tragic or joyful, neutrality will help you understand both the opportunities and the lessons. You'll realize that you have thoughts, desires, emotions, and feelings, but that none of these define who you are. Who you are, you'll begin to recognize, is a center of calm awareness, a quiet witness to life's drama. Personal problems will have less of a hold on you, and you'll develop the ability to simply watch your thoughts and feelings without attachment or suffering.

You purchase this precious neutral mind with the coin of meditative practice. Surely some degree of neutrality already exists in you. But to really develop your capacity to remain neutral and happy—no matter how life may challenge you— nothing is as effective as the practice of meditation.

Further meditative practice will give you still greater clarity. You will come to more fully understand your essential self and know that it can remain peaceful even as your emotions and surroundings go through their changes, even in the face of death itself. The inner self does not have a form in the sense that you can grasp it. This seer within you simply exists as a formless joy.

Ultimately, meditation and neutrality will serve you as a platform from which you can attain absolute freedom and realize the joy of total immersion in the "Now." Then you will discover, ironically, that this joyful consciousness has existed within you all the time, and that your desire for peace (like any other desire) had actually moved you away from peace. Other urges had substituted for your most fundamental urge. Every "reaching for" had pushed you away. Every move you made, no matter how lofty its intentions, had separated you from your self.

Success will eventually come to you, but not through hard work or desire. It will come, instead, through practice: the practice of doing nothing; the practice of offering zero resistance to the experience of the present moment; the practice of dropping all sense of separateness between your world and your self; the practice of letting body and mind drop away; the practice of simply being. This is the practice of meditation.

2

◗ THE ELEMENTS OF MEDITATION ◢

TUNING IN

t's hard to just sit down and start meditating after having spent the night
dreaming or, in the evening, having
just finished a busy day of work, classes, meetings
and the like. My teacher, Yogi Bhajan, always
taught me to tune in before any session of yoga or
meditation.

Tuning in helps to make sacred the time you

devote to your meditation, separating it from the normal rush of events and thoughts. It causes you to pause and, in a definite way, begin the meditative process. It gives you a chance to let go of thoughts and tension and to change your mood or mind-set. It causes you to redirect your energies towards meditation.

When you tune in to the infinite in this way, you set aside your limited self, personality, and ego in deference to a greater self, an unlimited self and its wisdom. At least for the duration of your meditation, you allow yourself to let go of your thoughts, desires, and emotions. Use the tuning-in process as a statement of purpose.

In Yogi Bhajan's teaching you sit straight, press your palms together in front of your chest, and take a long deep breath. Using that breath, chant the words Ong Namo Guru Dev Namo (I bow to the Creator of all things. I bow to its divine wisdom). Chant all the words on a single breath. Let your voice be clear and powerful. Repeat this three times or more. This chant (or mantra) will help keep you focused. This is demonstrated at the beginning of side one of the tape.

Other methods of tuning in also work well. The simplest might involve nothing more than taking three long deep breaths as you mindfully come into the here and now. A brief prayer or affirmation regarding the quality of your coming meditation will also work. Use whichever technique you wish.

SITTING

You can meditate sitting in a chair, or on the floor or ground. The best chair would not have cushions other than perhaps a little padding in the seat. A straight chair without arms works best. You will want to sit, if possible, without leaning against the back of the chair. Plant both feet flat on the floor about shoulder width apart, with your toes pointed straight ahead.

If you want to sit on the floor or ground

Figure 1

Figure 2

Figure 3

Figure 4

(which gives you the freedom to meditate any-where) you can sit cross-legged in what is called the full lotus position by placing your right foot on your left thigh and then placing your left foot on the right thigh (figure 1). Or, you can sit in the half lotus position with your right foot against your left thigh and your left foot on your right thigh (figure 2). You can also sit with your legs crossed in front of you without putting either foot onto your thighs (figure 3). Finally, you can sit in the rock pose by sitting solid as a rock on both of your heels (figure 4).

Whichever sitting posture you choose should serve to align your spine in a straight though relaxed way. Sit upright without leaning to either the left or right, front or back. Your ears should align over your shoulders, and your nose directly over your navel.

If you sit on the floor, first put down a firm pad, preferably made of natural materials. You can use several layers of Turkish towels, a small wool carpet, or a sheepskin. Avoid plastic or foam rubber mats, or anything overly thick and soft. To make yourself more comfortable, you can sit on the front edge of a small, firm pillow. This will lift the base of your spine higher than your knees and will help maintain you in a stable upright posture. If you sit on your heels, you may appreciate a firm pillow between your legs and under the base of your spine to take the pressure off your knees and feet. Whichever posture you choose, strive for comfort, stability, and a straight spine. These will become quite important to you if you meditate for more than a few minutes. Good posture helps quiet mental noise and helps lead you to stillness and tranquillity. On the other hand, nothing interferes with meditation as easily as a pain in your knee or neck, so find the posture that works best for you and stick with it. Slowly, with regular practice, it should become more and more comfortable.

HAND POSITIONS

In describing some of the individual meditations in chapter three, I'll teach you specific hand positions. These have subtle effects on your body and mind, much like pushing on an accupressure point might. With one or two exceptions, you can use any of these hand positions with any of the meditations. Find what seems most comfortable and natural for you, but do use one of them. It will help you as you strive to increase in neutrality and focus.

EYE FOCUS

Visual focus has enormous influence on meditation. If your eyes wander, your mind will constantly react to what they see. Conversely, if your eyes focus (either internally or externally), your mind will automatically slow down its chatter. One way to focus consists of closing your eyes, gently crossing them and rolling them back as if you were looking at your third eye of wisdom and intuition, the point on the inside of your skull at the center of your brow (many of the Eastern traditions consider the third eye to be the seat of the soul). Don't expect to see anything there, and don't strain your eye muscles. Just use gentle pressure to keep your eyes focused there.

Alternatively, you can have your eyes just barely open and slightly crossed and gaze at the tip of your nose. Or you can let your eyes remain open, but keep them in a soft focus, gazing down at the floor or ground in front of you.

Looking at your third eye or at the tip of your nose will direct your attention inward towards your spiritual self. The soft focus outside your self promotes an equal awareness of all things. Pick what seems easiest and most comfortable for you. Just remember that looking around you will very effectively stop the meditation process.

BREATH

Most people don't know how to breathe. They take in enough air to sustain life, but they breathe with short, shallow breaths. That sort of breath goes hand in hand with tension and mental agitation. By learning to breathe effortlessly in long, slow and deep breaths, you will automatically create relaxation of mind and body. Breathe calmly and your mind will calm.

Most of us have forgotten how to breathe naturally. Start each breath by filling the lower part of your lungs first, slowly dropping the diaphragm (the strong, flat muscle that separates the chest from the abdomen) and expanding your belly. After your belly reaches an almost full expansion, begin to expand and lift your rib cage. Finally, your collar bones spread up and out a bit to complete the filling of your lungs. To exhale, breathe out from the top all the way down. Let your ribs drop first and then pull in your belly (lifting the diaphragm) to finish emptying your lungs. Reread this paragraph several times as you follow the descriptions with your own breath. Many people have trouble with this at first. They think of a deep breath as an exaggerated expansion of their chest and hardly use their diaphragm at all. Practice. Proper breathing has enormous value.

Figure 5

To practice breathing sit comfortably erect, with loose clothing. Place one palm flat on your belly over your navel, with the other hand over your heart (figure 5). During normal relaxed breathing the hand over your navel should move in and out two or three times as much as the hand over your heart. In a long deep inhale the belly hand should move out to the maximum before the chest hand starts to move out at all. On the exhale the chest goes in completely before the belly begins to contract. You might feel uncoordinated with this at first. Just keep it up. The effort you make to relearn correct breathing will pay you back many times over in calmness and clarity.

As you relax further into this new breath pattern try to breathe even more completely. On the inhale feel the expansion in your lower back as well as your belly and then let your rib cage expand up and to the sides as well as forward. This breath doesn't have to be heavy, but it should use the entire breathing apparatus. Once in a while, to check your progress, time your breath.

21

At about eight breaths per minute (or fewer), the automatic relaxing effect of slow breathing takes hold. The slower your breathing, the more calm your mind will become. Notice the condition of your mind and the condition of your breath at the same moment, and you will see the relationship between them. Deep, gentle, rhythmic and slow breath correlates with peaceful, relaxed, mental states. And when your breath reaches a state of extreme stillness, your sixth sense (your intuition) begins to automatically awaken.

Don't limit proper breathing to your meditation practice sessions. Rather, try to notice and regulate your breath throughout the day. Begin by pausing for two or three long deep breaths before each meal. At work or study, or anytime you don't need to be talking, you can practice long deep breathing, slowly increasing the length and depth of each breath. Slowly but surely, full, deep, regular breathing will become your habit and natural pattern.

MANTRAS

> "In the beginning was the Word, and the
> Word was with God and the Word was
> God."

> Genesis

> "He who existed by Himself let first stream
> forth the eternal Word, without beginning or
> end."

> The Upanishads

Your mind thinks. And thinks and thinks. It never stops. It never will, not until your last breath. Beginning meditators often anguish over their non-stop thoughts. But to attempt to take the thought out of your mind has about as much chance of success as trying to take the wetness out of water. The mind must think. Every bit of sensory input (whether from the external world or from the body itself) sets up waves of thought, just as a stone dropped into a puddle creates ripples on the water's surface. Every thought then sets up new waves of thought. Emotions spring up in reaction to the thoughts, and these, in turn, engender still more thoughts and more emotions.

I sit at my desk now writing these words and I note many sensations. My right hand feels cold. I hear a tape playing in the next room. I see the clock face—12:30. My mind races: "The refrigerator repairman said he would be here between 12:00 and 2:00." "Should I move downstairs so I will hear his knock at the door?" "What a nuisance to have to deal with such mundane matters." "That refrigerator cost so much." [Back to my writing] ... "My foot hurts a bit, too much pressure there." [Shift position] "I wish I was in better shape; my body feels so stiff." "How will I ever age gracefully?" "Look—there—a blue jay outside my window, how lovely. God, I love springtime."

These thoughts took but a few seconds. In that same moment hundreds of others flashed by too fast to even register consciously. The thinking will not stop—ever—as long as I live. Then, how can one meditate? How does one achieve stillness?

One answer lies in the use of mantras. You cannot eliminate thought, but you can choose what you think about. A mantra serves you as a consciously chosen single thought. Repeated over and over, it replaces the thousands of random thoughts with just one thought. You choose this one thought, and it serves your purpose. This process works because of a unique characteristic of the mind. Although it can accommodate a hundred thoughts in the blink of an eye, the conscious mind processes these thoughts one at a time. Thus, by thinking only of the mantra there simply remains no room for other thoughts. Instead of going off in countless directions, your mind can focus in one direction. Freed from wave after wave of emotion-filled reactions, your mind can settle into unified action and focused mental effort.

Don't underestimate the power of this. Typically, we dissipate our mental energy. It spreads out in all directions at once like the light from a bulb. But with a mantra, the mind's energy can focus. When the energy of a single bulb is focused with a crystal in a particular way, it becomes a laser capable of even cutting steel. In the same way, when you focus your mental energy with a mantra, it becomes incredibly potent.

The focused mind can accomplish anything. All significant success requires focus. Successful business people, great artists, and skilled athletes all have developed their power to focus. By practicing meditation with a mantra you develop your ability to focus and the habit to do so. This skill will serve you in all other aspects of your life.

When you meditate, you have to meditate on something. Trying to empty the mind doesn't work. That cannot be done. Instead you can fill the mind with only a single thought. Most mantras consist of a single word or a brief phrase, often not in English. Think of them primarily as sound, as vibrations, as the very simplest of thoughts with the minimum of "content." You repeat a mantra over and over, linking its repetition to the rhythm of your breath (or perhaps to your pulse or to the rhythm of your stride as you walk). This simple thought replaces all other thoughts and leads you to a mental quietness.

The meaning of a mantra should relate to the purest, most universal, most infinite concepts. Since the mantra you repeat leads your consciousness, you want the mantra to refer to the highest and purest aspects of your self or reality.

If (to use a negative example) I were to choose as a mantra the word "dog" and to repeat it to the exclusion of other thought, my mind would certainly have less clutter than usual, and I would get some of the benefits of meditation. But, unless I aspire to manifest the attributes of a domesticated carnivorous pack animal, I would be well advised to meditate on something more lofty. I often use the mantra Sat Nam (pronounced "sut naam" and meaning "true name"). It refers to one's transcendent self or to one's true identity or soul. Like other mantras, Sat Nam refers to higher qualities and to the infinite. I will teach you other mantras in the instructions section (see pages 51-52).

Mantras have a vibrational nature. When you listen to the tape, you will hear mantras used in a way that causes physical and mental resonance in the meditator. Sound strongly affects consciousness, and certain sounds can help elevate consciousness. The human voice used in particular ways can create such elevating sounds. In practicing mantra meditation you will use mantras in this way. Allow yourself to hear and feel the sound. Create the sound with your voice (or hear it mentally) and allow that sound to carry you along like a boat might be carried by a current. Ride the waves of the sound, relaxing in the pure vibration of it, and it will uplift you.

CONCENTRATION

The word meditation actually refers to the state of mind that develops after a prolonged period of concentration. Concentration is the essence of meditation. Normally, your mental energy is scattered into a thousand directions, and the power of your mind dissipates just like the light from a lamp diffuses as it goes out in all directions at once. But, when the rays of light of that lamp focus into a beam we have a searchlight. In just the same way, the mind can focus on a single object, forgetting all else for a time. That object will come into sharp clarity, and you will see it in all its detail. Then, and only then, can you begin to truly know that object. Concentrate your mind on what you care about, and your understanding of that object will grow.

If you were to try to read a scientific article and, at the same time, paid attention to the tick of the clock, to your worries about your child's problem at school, as well as to endless other distractions, you would never get to understand the article you were reading.

Have you seen a cat stalk a bird? It fixes all its energy and attention in one direction. It exercises complete self-control. Only then does it have some chance of success.

When you sit down to meditate, you intentionally withdraw from the senses—and from past and future—and focus instead on the breath, on the here and now, on the mantra, or on some other object of contemplation. The distractions of extraneous input decrease, and your awareness of what you focus on increases.

Great souls have always told us, and you yourself will begin to know, that pure consciousness (unlike the body, mind, or personality) has an immortal nature. It exists, has existed, and will continue to exist beyond time and space, beyond body or mind. Through concentration you can become aware of this immortal self. You become immortal, not through some miraculous change or angelic transformation, but simply by becoming aware of an immortality that already exists.

Right now, at this very moment, you have immortality, but you do not have the consciousness of it. You do not feel it. Why? Simply because your senses have distracted you from that awareness.

Every bit of sensory input creates modifications or disturbances in your consciousness. Each disturbance makes you less able to perceive the true nature of reality, or of consciousness itself.

You must use the tool of concentration, the power of concentration, to withdraw your consciousness into itself. Then you will enter into the purest state of the neutral, meditative mind—a state where you can know by direct experience your immortal nature and the true nature of all reality.

As lofty as all this sounds, it need not be difficult to achieve such a state. You must simply hold your mind at one point for a long time. At first you might not succeed at this; your mind may seem to always run away, unstoppable. Like a broad deep river, the surface of your mind seems calm and smooth. Just dip below the surface, and you'll find currents there that cannot easily be checked. Don't worry. At first concentrate on the concrete form of your breath, the mantra, or the object of your concentration. Breathe in, breathe out, breathe in, breathe out. Sat Nam, Sat Nam, Sat Nam, over and over. Then, gradually, with your mind held on the concrete, you will go to the abstract nature of it. Instead of thinking "breathe" or "Sat Nam," you will experience a unity with it. You and the object of your concentration will become as one. We call this merging and this unity absorption. It exists only at the neutral point of meditation. At this point, in this state, you ask for nothing, and all desire slips away (including the desire for enlightenment or for God). Here you can simply be: at one with your highest nature.

RELAXATION

Both mind and body need periods of relaxation. Without relaxation you become progressively less efficient in your work. Without relaxation your happiness decreases, your crankiness increases, and you notice less of the subtle beauty of life. Without relaxation you eventually become exhausted, physically or emotionally. Most of us know how to make an effort to work for what we want, but few of us know how to really relax.

Relaxation may come as a side effect of recreation, but not necessarily so. Real relaxation, characterized by a complete letting go of all mental and physical tension, occurs only rarely.

Relaxation is the absence of tension. Tension builds in us when we react in a guarded self-protecting way to stressors and then don't release the tension when it no longer serves us. Tension certainly has a use. The well-known "fight or flight" mechanism that let our human race survive up until now depends on appropriate tension. The problem lies in the fact that we often don't know how or when to relax again. In modern society life keeps coming at us. Long hours at work, home and family responsibilities, illness, marital problems, and the daily world news all lead to tension. Work, extra curricular activities, meetings, and even our time at the health club all crowd into full schedules. All of us need periods of total relaxation, times when we do nothing, times when we have no purpose, times when we just allow ourselves to be.

When we give ourselves such time, several

benefits come to us. First, we release accumulated tension. When you do the guided relaxation on the tape you will experience this. It feels wonderful. The experience of deep relaxation calms, refreshes, and energizes both body and mind. Deep relaxation will leave you ready to go again, more able to do what you must.

A second benefit of practicing relaxation comes from learning exactly what it feels like to relax. Your mind and body will memorize that sensation. You'll come to crave the feeling of relaxation and only reluctantly give it up. After you have come to know relaxation, you will want that experience more and more. When face to face with one of the stressors of your life, you'll learn to choose relaxation instead of choosing tension.

Had you realized that you had that choice or did you believe that tension inevitably results from stress? The belief that chronic or accumulated tension must result from a stressful life parallels the equally erroneous view that happiness results from what happens to you. Neither idea has any truth in it. Happiness and relaxation result from choices and efforts you make.

Relaxation need not be reserved for when we feel especially stressed and tense. Relaxation can become a part of your regular daily practice. You will find that you begin to create a loop: relaxation leads to better meditation, and meditation leads to more relaxation. The relaxation will also carry over into the rest of your life, so stress will have less of an effect on you. Your practice of meditation will teach you to relax, and your relaxation practice will enhance your meditation. Have patience with this, and enjoy watching your own progress.

The meditation process consists of doing nothing other than remaining constantly aware, in a relaxed way, of the object of your meditation: breath, mantra, pure consciousness or whatever. That means that you allow all else to drop away, letting go of attachments and fears. How do you hold onto a fear? Through tension. How do you hold onto an attachment? With tension. How do you let go of these things? With relaxation. Tension is the holding of fear in the body or mind; relaxation occurs when you let it go.

Does this sound too simple? Do you want some complicated prescription? I don't have one. Practice with the tape, and the skill of relaxation will be yours. Use your will power, and that skill will set you free from useless tension. Eventually you will master relaxation, a most wonderful accomplishment. The further along that path you progress, the better you will experience meditation.

AFFIRMATIONS AND VISUALIZATIONS

Affirmations and visualizations both use the natural power of your imagination to intentionally create desirable mental and physical states. Everyone, every day, unintentionally creates his or her own mental states. Unfortunately, what you unintentionally create may lead to undesirable results.

Both affirmations and visualizations rely on this concept: before you can achieve anything you must first create the thought of that achievement. Just as a blueprint precedes the building, thoughts or ideas precede accomplishment. Whatever you steadfastly hold in your mind, whether positive or negative, will eventually manifest itself. This occurs on all levels. Slalom ski racers close their eyes and "see" themselves successfully negotiating the race course before they start their run. Patients who learn to visualize their own healing taking place have higher survival rates than those who assume they will die. School children who believe themselves to be capable do much better academically than those with low self-esteem.

Moreover, the stronger the belief, the more vivid the imagination, or the clearer the image, then the more powerful the effect. When we hold fearful or negative thoughts in our minds, we attract what we fear. When our expectations are positive, we attract the positive. Whatever we most believe, we manifest.

Perhaps you are ill and want to recover. You might "see" yourself healthy, engaged in vigorous activity. You might "hear" others' reactions to how healthy you have become. You might view your own strength returning and mentally experience yourself doing all those things you would do if you had perfect health.

The conscious process of visualization or affirmation requires more than superficial positive thought. Begin with sitting as for meditation and then deeply relax. Once relaxed, create in your mind a very complete thought of whatever you wish to manifest in your life.

Take as much time with this as you need. For example, create a very complete scenario of yourself in health. Once you have done that, hold that idea in your mind and contemplate it fully. Merge with the idea of it, and let that idea become a part of you. Then, create a statement about the desired situation, something that briefly describes it. You might say: "I have achieved a wonderful state of vibrant good health," as you continue to hold onto the visualization of that in your mind. Repeat that statement, your affirmation, over and over.

Possibly, negating thoughts will also arise in your mind, the "yeah, buts": "I have achieved a wonderful state of vibrant, good health. Yeah, but what about my diagnosis of _____? That could kill me." When these negating thoughts occur— and they will—don't fight them. Just allow them to pass through your mind like a cloud across the sky. Observe your thoughts, and let them go while continuing to repeat your affirmation.

Some thoughts will persist in opposition to your affirming and may need a different kind of attention. Staying with the example of illness, perhaps you do have only a slim chance of survival. Affirmations and visualizations around recovery should still be done, but they can be more customized to your situation. Create images of the exact physiological healing process required. Your health practitioner can help you understand this. There exists strong evidence that visualizing these healing processes can help the body heal even in extreme situations.

You would probably also benefit from additional visualizations that deal directly with the "yeah, but": visualizations in which you have peace, contentment, and emotional and spiritual healing, regardless of what might happen to you physically. If carefully constructed, such an image would not contradict the image of possible physical healing.

In deciding what to work on with these techniques, start with whatever seems fairly achievable. My example of healing from a serious illness might stretch your abilities too much in the beginning. If you actually have such an illness you might want to start with smaller, more easily achievable goals. Later, with some experience and confidence, you could take on bigger challenges.

Let yourself get quite clear about your goals. The more specific the better. Fill in your visualization with lots of realistic and achievable detail, and use all your senses. See, hear, feel, even taste and smell the results you wish to achieve.

Come back to your visualizations and affirmations often. Once you have done a few formal sessions, just repeating the affirmation from time to time throughout the day will boost your progress. Do this especially when you notice your mind dwelling on fears or negativity.

In composing affirmations, several rules will help you make the most powerful statements. First, affirmations contain only positive words. Avoid saying things such as: "I won't fail" or "I'm not afraid." The subconscious mind seems not to register the negative word and instead picks up only the "fail" or "afraid."

Second, affirmations occur now, in the present. Tomorrow never comes. Statements like: "I am going to earn $5,000 more next year" or "My relationship with my son will become more loving" allow the subconscious mind to postpone to another time the change that needs to occur now. Instead say: "I am earning. . . ." or "I am lovingly relating. . . ."

Third, positive emotional terms add punch to the power of an affirmation: "I am loving how relaxed my neck muscles are," or "I am proudly and confidently accepting my new job offer."

Finally, if you are religiously or spiritually inclined, consider adding reference to the source of all the goodness in your life: "Because of God's abundance, I am easily and gladly paying all my debts without any financial strain," or "The infinite wisdom of the universe flows through me, and I am joyfully knowing and accepting what I must do."

As these words are spoken, your mind may produce contradictory thoughts. Just observe them, or modify your affirmation to cover the questions raised. When you repeat your affirmation "I enjoy my job," you might hear a little voice saying: "Yes, I would—if it weren't for my boss' unreasonable demands." If so, you could change the affirmation to: "I am enjoying my job. When my boss asks a lot of me, I gladly respond with enthusiastic effort." If another thought comes through such as: "Nothing I could do would satisfy that creep," an affirmation of: "I am opening new opportunities for myself because of my high quality and enthusiastic work," might be appropriate. Notice the new thrust towards a different job. The process of evolving the affirmation to account for the "Yeah, buts" has shown the need for a new direction. Now a new visualization will also be needed, perhaps one that pictures you in a different, more rewarding job.

This process can continue indefinitely as your life evolves towards the achievement of your destiny. Just be sure that you keep tapping into your higher self. Affirmations and visualizations coming out of negative emotions won't go anywhere. Remember also that you can't have or shouldn't have certain things or that some things can only come to you at some other time. Meditation used just to get more of what you want, or to try to force something that can't or shouldn't happen, won't work. Your mind and body will only tense at the suggestion. If you seem stalled with this whole process, just back off. Do simple meditation, and slow yourself down. Contact your inner self. Maybe it wants something quite different (and better) for you.

COMING OUT OF YOUR MEDITATION

At the end of your practice time, don't jump up and immediately get back into busyness. Doing so causes you to miss out on some of meditation's greatest rewards. It can shock your nervous system and leave you with the subtle message that meditation leads to an uncomfortable reentry into normal activity.

When you have finished a meditation, take a long deep breath. Hold this breath for ten seconds or more; then slowly let it go. Repeat that two or three times, holding the breath as long as you comfortably can. Let the mantra, if you are using one, just echo in your mind.

Then sit, gently focused and perfectly still. In the stillness of this moment, which you can stretch out for as long as you wish, may come the most profound experience of your meditation, the closest contact with your higher self. Feel the profound peace of it. Let the stillness last and last, and listen to whatever inner voices may come to you. Finally, the time to end the meditation session will come. Take another deep breath, and while you hold it for a few seconds, vigorously rub your palms together, or reach up over your head and shake your hands. This will get you "grounded" again and will help your mind and body reconnect with one another.

Then, if at all possible, just relax for a little while before getting up and resuming your day's activities. If you have meditated with others, try to limit your conversation to uplifting topics.

All of this serves to extend your meditation into the rest of your life. Ultimately you want to develop a full-time meditative mind, one which remains neutral and fully aware throughout the day. Instead of stopping the meditative process, these simple ways of exiting the formal meditation and easing back into the other activities of life help bring the meditative mind into "real life."

You need to maintain a balance here. You don't want to be "spaced out" as you try to drive your car or figure out your income taxes. Therefore, you definitely do come out of the meditations. Yet you want the neutrality and peace of mind that the meditation gives, so you hold onto these attributes even while not actually meditating. Practice will allow you to keep this balance. It will probably prove easy enough to come out of the meditation, but it will take some conscious effort to bring the lessons of meditation into your everyday life.

3

❧ THE MEDITATIONS ❧

Let's begin with the relaxation exercise. When you use the tape my voice will guide you through a sequence, progressively relaxing first one part of your body, and then another. Once your whole body has relaxed, I'll guide you so you can deepen your relaxation by letting go of your sensory awareness. Before helping you return to a more normal state, I will make some suggestions about how easily you can return to this deeply relaxed state in the future whenever you want to do so.

To end the relaxation sequence (which will take a total of about fifteen minutes), I'll help you lighten your relaxation step by step. Finally, I'll have you take a few deep breaths and do some very simple body movements to get you fully alert again.

DEEP RELAXATION

Before turning on the tape, you should be sure that nothing will disturb you during the exercise. Ask others not to come into the room, unplug the phone, etc.

Be sure you will be physically comfortable. Either sit in a supportive chair such as a lounger, or lie flat on your back on the floor or in bed. Perhaps your neck or back will require you to use a pillow for support. Cover yourself with a blanket if the air feels cool. Provide all this before beginning the tape.

Just before turning on the tape, say out loud: "I will deeply relax with this tape, yet when the relaxation is over I will again be fully alert." This will keep you from falling asleep and missing the next thing in your day's schedule.

In case you want to fall asleep after relaxing, I have put this relaxation sequence last on side one of the tape. That way, if you wish, you can go through this sequence before sleep and just let the tape turn off by itself. If you choose to do that, just before starting the tape, say: "I will deeply relax with this tape. When the instructions say to come out of the relaxation, I will instead enter into a deep and restful sleep and reawaken refreshed at ___ o'clock."

The tape should not only relax you, but should also teach you how to relax yourself. Use the tape a few times; listen to it once without relaxing to be sure you consciously have heard it all; then try to do a deep relaxation on your own—without the tape. Mastering this has several advantages. First, you'll be able to use the technique any time and any place. I've had people tell me stories of forgetting their tape when they have gone on trips and not being able to enjoy their vacation! They felt as tense as they used to before they began to use a relaxation tape. You'll want to avoid that sort of dependency.

Second, you'll be able to use the relaxation sequence without disturbing your bed partner or the person next to you on the airplane. Mastering the skill of relaxation allows you to do little spot relaxations whenever you notice tension: during a meeting, perhaps, or before a sports competition.

Third, without the tape, you can begin to customize your relaxation. When you have gotten yourself into a deeply relaxed state, you can talk to yourself with affirmations, or ask yourself questions such as "What do I need to do to rid myself of this illness?" or "What path will lead me to the greatest happiness in life?" Positive questions like these, asked of your higher awareness, get answers. The practice consists of simply relaxing yourself, assuming you have a considerable reserve of untapped wisdom, and while asking it for help, assuming you will receive it. The more you ask of your higher Self, the more you will receive.

But first things first. Practice with the tape for awhile. Then, use the relaxed state as a beginning, rather than as an end in itself. Relaxation remains one of the fundamental cornerstones of meditation, success, health, and happiness. Master the art of relaxation, and you will begin to master yourself.

Before entering deep relaxation, or any of the meditations, tune in (see pages 11–13). To do so, I use the mantra Ong Namo Guru Dev Namo repeated three times. This tuning in is demonstrated in the beginning of side one of the tape.

SILENT MEDITATION: ANY MANTRA

I've already explained the mantra Sat Nam. Literally, it means means "truth name." Figuratively, it translates as "true identity" (one's innermost self), or as "God is truth," or as "God's Name is truth." When doing this silent meditation, any mantra will work equally well. If Sat Nam doesn't appeal to you choose one from the list below, or any others you may have learned elsewhere. Making up your own mantra can't hurt, but those listed here have a certain effective rhythm and a vibrational quality that does not occur with just any words. I've given the mantra, its origin, and meaning.

> *Sat Nam* (Gurumukhi: "God is Truth or True Identity")
> *I am*
> *Wahe Guru* (Gurumukhi: "Indescribable wisdom")
> *Ong* (Gurumukhi: "Creator pervading all Creation")
> *Healthy am I; Happy am I; Holy am I*
> *God and Me, Me and God, Are One*
> *Ribbono Shel Olam* (Hebrew: "Master of the Universe")
> *Lord Jesus Christ, Son of God, Have Mercy on Me*
> *Om* or *Aum* (Sanskrit: "Existential multiplicity and its underlying reality"
> *Svaha* (Sanskrit: "Hail")
> *Tat Tvam Asi* (Sanskrit: "That Thou Art")
> *Allah Ahkba* (Islam: "God is Great")
> *La Illa Ha Illa Allah Ho* (Islam: "There is nothing but God")
> *Aum Maanpayme Hum* (Buddhism: "Hail to the thought of one's own Enlightened Being")

For this silent meditation sit either on a

chair or on the floor. Straighten your spine. Draw your chin straight back. Elevate your chest a bit, and pull your shoulders back slightly. The posture should feel like standing at attention, but without any rigidity or strain. Let your hands rest on your knees, with your palms facing upward. Hold the tip of your index fingers lightly against the tip of your thumbs, with your other fingers straight but, again, not rigid.

Let a tiny part of your mind remain aware of your body posture throughout this meditation. Try to avoid slouching, leaning forward or back, or to either side. Picture yourself, and feel yourself as strong, yet relaxed.

Your breathing for this meditation will consist of inhaling in two breaths, followed by exhaling in one breath. Inhale to fill your abdomen. Feel the expansion of it in your back and sides, as well as in your belly. Hold it. Do not exhale. Then, with a completely separate second breath, also expand your chest. Your rib cage should expand out and up, and even your collar bones

should lift up a bit. The two inhalations will completely fill your lungs. Between these two separate
breaths, pause about one second. Pause for another
second after the second breath. Then let out all
the air in one long exhalation that should last as
long as the two inhalations together. Again, pause
for one second before beginning the next breath
in. This whole sequence should take a minimum
of eight to ten seconds. With practice, you might
be able to stretch this out to as much as twice that
length of time or to a rate of about three or four
breaths per minute. While doing this, focus on
your third eye, or on the tip of your nose, as you
wish.

Pick the mantra you want to use, and coor-
dinate it with the breathing. The three longer
mantras that I have given in English are divided
into three parts already. Inhale with the first part,
inhale with the second part, and exhale with the
third. This means that as you take in the first
breath, you will mentally "hear" or "feel" the
sound of the first part of the mantra. This will

happen again with the second part of the mantra. The third part of the mantra will occur as you breathe out. Some people do better at "seeing" the words written in front of their mind's eye. You want the mantra to replace other thoughts. In whatever way you experience the mantra, just keep it prominent in your mind: hearing it, feeling it, or seeing it. It doesn't matter which. Let the mantra "fill" your mind.

If you want to use one of the other mantras given, or one that you know from another source, you can divide it into three parts or repeat it three times, or you can use a combination of two mantras. For example: "I am" [inhale], "I am" [inhale], "Sat Nam" [exhale]. Or "Sat" [inhale], "Nam" [inhale], "Wahe Guru" [exhale].

On the tape you will hear a summary of these instructions, and I will also put in an occasional reminder for you to repeat your mantra. At a certain point in your development, these reminders may feel like more of an interruption of your concentration than a help. When that happens, or when you want to extend the time of your practice, begin to meditate without the tape.

At the end of this meditation, take a long deep breath and hold it for awhile. Then relax the breath, and sit in perfect stillness (you may need to turn off the tape so you won't be disturbed by the start of the next meditation). During this time your mantra will continue to echo in your mind. Aim for absolute mental and physical silence, and just listen to the "sound" of the mantra within that silence. Stretch out this delicious moment for as long as you wish, and then come out of the meditation as described on pages 44–45.

SITTING ZAZEN

The Soto School of Zen Buddhists have given us Zazen, the experience of life without ego, without interpretation, perhaps the simplest of meditative practices. To practice Zazen, simply sit with awareness. To the Zen practitioner, no one thing has more value than another. A Zen voice would say that everything has equal sanctity—or that nothing has any at all. In ordinary life we normally see everything with a subjective eye; thus all appears in terms of duality: good vs. bad, life vs. death, friend vs. foe, cold vs. warm, liberated vs. enslaved. We occupy ourselves with constant judgments and thinking about things.

In Zazen you replace thinking about with the direct experience of reality. You sit yourself in the middle of good and evil, past and future and there you experience your self, your underlying nature, your Buddha nature. Zen Buddhists recognize that you already have a Buddha nature. Sitting Zazen expresses that.

To sit Zazen, have a quiet room. As with other meditation, it helps to have an empty stomach and to leave as much of your agitation as you can outside of the room. It also helps to leave outside any thoughts of success or failure with meditation.

Sit in one of the postures described on pages 13–15. Rest your right hand on your lap with your palm up. Place your left hand on top of your

Figure 6

right with the tips of your thumbs lightly touching. Sit straight without leaning forward, backward, or sideways (figure 6). In the beginning, you might want to ask someone to check your sitting posture or check it for yourself in a mirror.

Lightly press your tongue against your palate and close your lips and teeth together, also lightly. Let your eyes remain half open, in soft focus. Gaze down in front of you at about a 45 degree angle. Breathe through your nose, taking one or two long deep breaths to tune in. Then sit firmly, with your breath relaxed.

Begin your practice by mentally counting your breaths. While inhaling count "one," while exhaling count "two." On the next inhale count "three" and so on—up to ten. Then begin again with "one." This gives your mind nothing to feed on. If you lose track of your counting, just begin again. When breathing, don't think "I breathe." In that phrase, the "I" is extra. Simply follow, with awareness, the movement of your breathing.

Did I say "simply?" You will probably find

this a genuine challenge. You are asked to do virtually nothing, but your life-long habits of thought and activity don't simply switch off. You may still your body. A rock solid posture will help with that (although even this will require more practice than you might imagine). But stilling your mind?! That attempt may totally frustrate you. Don't even try. You haven't a chance. You can, however, just watch your mind. Aim for that. If you must be something, be an observer, looking at all things alike, following the movement of breath and mind, accepting equally what you like and what you don't like. Give up insisting on certain conditions. Recognize everything that you think or feel as a part of your true self. Therein lies your path.

Thoughts will come, and you may even totally forget the counting of breaths. Never mind. Just resume the practice, beginning at "one" again, without judging yourself. Whenever you notice a thought, visualize "putting it into the palms of your hands." With practice your mind will be quiet. Your life will feel more sane, and your loves and passions will begin to shine through.

Eventually, you will come to a point where you can leave behind even the simple practice of watching the breaths. Then you can practice Shikan-taza (practice-enlightenment). In Shikan-taza your mind will become like your body—firm, immovably rooted, at peace, and unhurried. You will feel an effortless and yet completely concentrated awareness. The great Zen master Dogen described this state of intense awareness as being like the vigilance of a swordsman in a duel. Let your mind become an unmoving center around which all else moves. See the truth everywhere. Come face to face with reality.

At the end of your practice period, slowly move your body, and calmly stand up. Take your free, yet concentrated mind with you as you go about ordinary life. The Zen Buddhist does not make a split between practice and life. Carry your practice with you wherever you go.

SA-TA-NA-MA MEDITATION

We will turn now to a chanting meditation, one in which you will use your voice to create a mantra on which you will meditate. The combined sound, vibration and rhythm of the mantra will have a positive effect on your mind. The sound of the chanted mantra acts like a link between your individual mind and the universal mind. With the mantra, you intentionally project out beyond yourself and towards the infinite (or deep within to the infinity that lies there). Mantra meditation gives you a most efficient technique to aim yourself at your ultimate destination.

In this particular meditation, you will use several different levels of sound with the mantra Sa Ta Na Ma. The Sa Ta Na Ma mantra breaks Sat Nam (truth manifested) into its component parts. Sa means "infinity, the very beginning." Ta means "life, existence." Na means "death", and Ma means "rebirth" or "resurrection." The "a" sound common to all four of these sounds (and to many other mantras) can be thought of or heard as the sound of the universe itself. Together, the sounds form a complete spectrum of primal sounds and represent the entire cycle of creation.

First chant the mantra aloud in your worldly human voice, using your tongue to form the sounds. Here the mantra will have a very physical nature. Next, switch to a more mental sound, a whisper made more in your throat. You will recognize this sound as the voice of a lover, the embodiment of your heart's yearning for higher consciousness. Then, switch to a silent repetition of the mantra using a non-audible "sound" formed mentally. This "sound" will come from the silence of your deeper spiritual self. Return to the whisper, and finally come back to your full voice.

Chant in each voice for equal time periods. For example, you might do two minutes aloud, two minutes whispering, two minutes silently, and then two more silently, two whispering, and end with two minutes aloud. These times (which we use on the tape) can be stretched out to five minutes for each division or even more. In the absolute silence that follows the meditation, listen for the sound of silence: the unstuck melody even beyond the mantra.

In all chanted mantras the total effect is enhanced by clear enunciation. The tongue, lips, and palate come into contact in specific ways and thus create subtle effects on mind and body. Many people tend to slur a mantra when chanting, creating an unclear, "spacy" sound. Do just the opposite, making crisp, clear tones.

As the mantra is chanted, touch the tips of your four fingers in turn to the tip of your thumb. This directs the power of the meditation to enhance different aspects of your consciousness and personality. On the sound of Sa touch your thumb to your index finger for intuition, mental expansion, and calmness. Touch your middle finger to your thumb on Ta for patience and the responsibility needed to keep to your duty. On Na touch your fourth finger, or ring finger, to your thumb for vitality, energy, and good health. Then, on Ma, touch your little finger to your thumb for the capacity to communicate clearly.

On the tape you will hear how we chant this mantra, but I note it here for those who can read music:

SA TA NA MA

Imagine that the sound enters your head straight down from above, and that you project it out at your third eye point (a half inch above the center of your eyebrows). The movement of the sound happens with each syllable, on Sa, on Ta, on Na, and again on Ma. By concentrating on this L-shaped movement of the sound energy, you will remain aware of the top of your head (associated with understanding and knowledge) and the third eye (associated with imagination and intuition).

For this meditation, close your eyes and gently cross them and roll them up, focusing at your third eye point. All meditation connects your limited self to your infinite self, linking the ordinary with the extraordinary. This Sa Ta Na Ma meditation does this by bringing you into a total mental balance, and by letting you know the world in its reality. When you have completed the meditation, sit in silence, experiencing the peace and the inner stillness of the moment.

You can do this meditation together with your partner, as a couple, by sitting back to back with your spines in contact over their whole length (figure 7). This practice will help eliminate fears in your relationship and open deeper communication. At the end of the session push your backs firmly together for a minute or so. Do this, and nothing will come between you!

Figure 7

MEDITATION FOR PROSPERITY

After all the discussion about remaining neutral and desireless, it may seem contradictory that I now offer a meditation with a goal, especially the goal of prosperity. Prosperity doesn't necessarily mean great wealth. Prosperity refers to that state in which you receive what you need through your own righteous effort, you give to others without hesitation a part of what you have, and you feel confident that the whole process of receiving and sharing shall continue. You develop an attitude of prosperity, an expectation of abundance in your life. Expect an abundance of joy, kindness, wisdom, love, and forgiveness first, and material things second.

But where does that belief in abundance come from? If you have had good fortune in life it may come from your experience. Life has always treated you well, and you may simply expect that you will continue to have loving, supportive relationships, peace of mind, and financial security. In fact, your expectation helps to insure your prosperity. Your whole life acts as a giant affirmation, and your past experiences tend to replicate themselves in the present and future.

If your past has not lived up to such an ideal, your expectations, your conditioning, might create an opposite tendency. Faced with a need, you might assume it will persist unmet. You might not take, or even notice, opportunities that present themselves to you. And you might not create your own opportunities.

Most meditations give you the experience of your own completeness. This meditation will do that, but it will also help you to set direction and develop your willingness to have. This ability allows you to accept goodness and positive people into your life. It allows you to feel comfortable with abundance.

It also will help you to understand the relationship between being (the experience you gain through meditation) and having (accepting into your life what you need). Most people make the mistake of believing that what they have will determine how they feel, or their state of being. They live backwards, assuming that the more they have, the better they will feel. Work on your state of being first. This will ultimately lead you to having what you need and what you truly want.

Examine your own beliefs. Do you believe that life necessarily includes suffering? Do you see some measure of nobility in poverty? Do you believe that the demands of the world's human population outweigh the planet's ability to supply those needs? These beliefs all follow the scarcity model: "Without enough to go around, only the greedy get what they want and everyone else suffers." Yet, despite the existence of the realities of poverty, starvation, and environmental degradation, we do have enough to go around—if we would but shift our priorities. This planet of ours can supply our needs renewably, with a fair share for all.

The non-material needs we have can also be met. There are no external limits to happiness or fulfillment in life. Everyone could have these in abundance—now. Try to drop the scarcity model, and understand the possibility of a universal prosperity and happiness.

Accept with grace and gratitude whatever does come to you. Do you believe you deserve prosperity? Could you actually accept what you want, or would that require remaking your self-image? Do you have the will to accept success and fulfillment?

Limitations in these attitudes often correlate with parallel limitations about self-worth. Can you say, without hesitation, the words: "I like myself, and I accept myself as I am?" You may need to work on developing these attitudes of self-love and deservedness.

To have and to maintain your abundance, you also need a desire and a willingness to give. When we believe in scarcity we tend to hold onto what we have. But, if you truly believe in abundance, giving comes naturally as a pleasure. This creates space for more receiving. The more you share, the more it seems your own dreams are fulfilled. Giving doesn't just imply gifts or donations. You can also give your love or expressions of gratitude, your time or your kindness. In whatever way you give, know that it insures your own further prosperity.

If you have any trouble with these attitudes, or any reluctance to accept these premises, this may tend to limit your prosperity. At the completion of the meditation I am about to describe, in that exquisite moment of stillness, clearly visualize yourself as prosperous. Feel the security of it, and imagine the fulfillment of your real needs. Take all the time necessary to develop this in your own mind. Then use an appropriate affirmation: "I am completely open and willing to receive all good and prosperity in my life," "I thoroughly enjoy both giving and receiving," or "I now receive all the money that I need." Refer back to pages 36–44 for guidelines to forming potent affirmations, and carefully examine your own attitudes to assure that your affirmations hit the target.

Now, finally, to the meditation itself. This

Figure 8

one works on developing your intuition so that you can know your inner calling. Knowing exactly what you must do in life should precede goal setting and action plans. This meditation will help you establish your personal vision so that you will know where to aim your effort. This meditation creates a space in which you will sense your own destiny. Do this over and over, each time getting deeper understanding and further insight. The meditation serves you like a compass on a foggy day at sea, constantly showing you the direction you must go in to reach your destination.

Begin by sitting comfortably with a straight spine. Tune in. Let your eyes close almost all the way and look with soft focus at the tip of your nose. Place your hands, palms up, with your right hand resting on the top of your left in a relaxed way at your navel point. Cross them at about a 45 degree angle to each other, with your thumb tips touching (figure 8).

Inhale deeply and fully, using both your diaphragm and rib cage, but divide the breath into eight separate and equal sniffs of air. By the eighth breath your lungs should have reached their capacity. Then, exhale while chanting the mantra Wahe Guru (Indescribable Wisdom) out loud, giving each sound equal emphasis. Pronounce the three parts of the mantra clearly, separating the sounds from one another. By the end of Guru you will have used all the air. Repeat this for eleven minutes or more.

As you do this, let the sound vibrate within your skull. Hear it, and feel it. Especially experience the sound near the top of your head. Imagine it awakening your intelligence and intuition to the possibilities life holds for you. Your neutral and balanced posture frees you from the concerns of your personal self. The total effect allows for the smaller self to reconnect with the greater self, for your finite to serve your infinite. That begins the elevation of your life so you live up to your highest purpose.

Your life has led you to the point you find yourself at today. You know that you have not yet finished. Your future awaits you. Greatness lies ahead, but exactly where? At the end of this meditation, sit and ask the question: "How shall I live up to my highest calling in life?" or whatever question seems most appropriate to you. Repeat your question several times. Ask from your heart, and listen with your heart. Listen carefully. The answer sometimes comes in the quietest of whispers, or in subtle symbols. It may not come right now, so just keep asking, repeating this meditation daily. Open yourself to understanding, and understanding will come. After a while, you may notice that things have changed in your life. Some opportunities have come along, you have become more content with some part of your life, or you feel strangely drawn to something new. Start the voyage. Follow the signs. Take along some courage—it may prove necessary at certain points along the way.

Come back to this meditation whenever you feel the need to restart the cycle of prosperity. That cycle always begins with stillness, potential,

Figure 9

and understanding. It begins with the sense of destiny and vision. This meditation is yours to keep. Use it well.

MEDITATION TO RELIEVE TENSION

Did you have a hard day today? This next meditation will fix you right up. It reverses your personal brain drain. It energizes and balances you. It is also an excellent meditation just before bed because its effects will help you relieve tension and sleep more peacefully.

Begin as always by tuning in. Sit comfortably and solidly, with your hands together, a few inches out from your navel area, fingers interlocked, with the index finger of each hand extended up and out at a 60 degree angle (figure 9). Don't cross your thumbs; hold them parallel to each other.

Take a deep breath, and chant a powerful ONG sound (the sound of infinity). Inhaling takes about five seconds, and the ONG sound is held as long as you are comfortably able to. As you get used to the breathing, you should lengthen each breath. The slower the better—as long as you are not struggling with the breath. If you do this meditation with others in a group, let each person chant it at his or her own speed, thus creating a continuous group sound. Do this with your eyes closed and focused at your third eye or brow point, your point of spiritual consciousness and intuition.

Sense yourself as balanced and energetic. Dwell on those feelings. Expand them. Really feel them. Sometimes you just have to pretend for a bit, until they become reality. This meditation has real power. Within a minute or so, you will feel the difference as you begin to experience your essence.

ONG! The sound of infinity stimulates the brain. You will feel the vibration in your soft palate and nose. The sound should resonate like a gong, so create a rich and full tone. The word ONG refers to the creator within all of creation.

A related and well-known mantra is OM

(the absolute, the void). The manifestation of that absolute, the creator as experienced within the creation, is what we call ONG.

With this meditation you will build a bridge of sound from yourself to the creator within you. Use this ONG meditation to establish a link between your personal self and your essence or transpersonal self.

4

🍂 FURTHER AIDS
TO MEDITATION 🍂

After tuning in at the beginning of each of your meditation sessions, you may want to do more to get ready to meditate. If you feel a need for more calmness, try this: sit straight, focus at your third eye and just concentrate there for up to five minutes. Then, raise your arms all the way over your head, and stretch. Imagine energy coming into your palms as you slowly turn your hands from left to right. Don't rotate your hands in circles; just move them back and forth. Keep up a gentle stretch in your arms. After two or three minutes, inhale completely, exhale completely, and relax your arms down. You will feel very calm and ready to meditate.

If you'd like to deepen your concentration, try this simple exercise: just before beginning your meditation, sit for three minutes with your eyes wide open but focused cross-eyed at the tip of your nose. Also, open your mouth wide and keep your tongue curled back, with the tip pressed hard against the back of your palate. This might look strange, but when you are done you will appreciate how much it helps you concentrate. You can also switch into this, for a minute or so, in the middle of a silent meditation if you find your mind wandering excessively.

BREATH

Breathing exercises will also help prepare

you for meditation. Here's one basic breathing method that I find very effective: sit comfortably and then take a long slow deep breath. Hold the breath while pulling in on your navel. This pull should move your navel in, perhaps two inches or more. Try to focus this pull just at your navel, rather than sucking in your whole belly. Hold the breath for five seconds or more. Exhale, and again pull in on your navel while holding the breath out for a time equal to the time that you held it in. Continue breathing this way, perhaps increasing the time you hold the breath, as you develop your capacity to do so. Keep this up for at least three minutes.

A powerful variation of this is to do twenty-six such breaths, one for each of your vertebrae, before starting your meditation. Concentrate on each vertebrae, one at a time, moving up your spine. This will bring you to a full alertness while centering your attention on your higher self. To add still more power to this, increase the length of time you hold the breath as much as possible, taking as much as one minute per breath.

To make this breathing exercise even more effective, use a mantra throughout. Inhale as you do four repetitions of the mantra. Hold the breath for eight repetitions of the mantra. Exhale for four more repetitions, and hold the breath out as you repeat the mantra another eight times. Build this up over time. The slower you breathe, the better.

YOGA

Nothing prepares you for meditation better than yoga. Yoga means "to yoke or unite." Through yoga you unite your lower self to your higher self, your finite body to your infinite soul. Yoga, originally developed in ancient India, works on many levels. It prepares the body to sit still for long periods without discomfort. It builds the nervous system, shielding you against the negative effects of stress. It stimulates the glandular system, a major regulator of body and mind. It develops inner strength and outer projection to protect you from unwanted negative influences.

To get a little feel of yoga, and to get ready for meditation, try these three simple exercises. First tune in (pages 11–13). Then, for the first exercise sit either on the front edge of a straight chair, or cross legged on the floor, holding your knees with your hands. Arch your lower spine forward as you inhale (with your diaphragm only), and let your spine back into a slump as you exhale. Keep your head and shoulders relatively still. Do this with your eyes closed, focused on your third eye. As you inhale, mentally repeat the sound SAT and as you exhale, mentally repeat the sound NAM (or use another mantra). Continue this forward and back motion for three minutes. Do it slowly in the beginning. As you get comfortable with the exercise, pick up speed to about one flex per second. Try to be loose with this, creating a nice fluid motion as you gradually loosen up your lower spine. For a slight variation of this exercise, hold your knees with your hands, and lock your elbows straight. This will move the center of the flex a little higher up your back. At the end of three minutes inhale deeply. Hold the breath for twenty seconds or so, then exhale and just meditate silently for one more minute.

For the second exercise also sit. Hold your upper arms straight out to the side, parallel to the floor, and bend your elbows so that your forearms are perpendicular to the floor. Then, while inhaling, rotate your whole torso, shoulders, and head to the left. While exhaling, rotate to the right. As before, concentrate on your third eye, and inhale and exhale with your mantra. Breathe with your diaphragm only. Keep this up for another three minutes. At the end, take a deep breath. Come to the center facing forward, and hold the breath for twenty seconds. Exhale, relax your arms, and meditate for one minute. As with the previous exercise, go for a nice loose movement and pick up speed as you become comfortable with the motion, moving at approximately two seconds for each repetition of the exercise.

For the third exercise, stand up. While

inhaling, raise your arms up over your head as high as possible. Then, as you exhale, bend forward from your waist, stretching your hands down towards your toes without bending your knees. Continue to inhale up and exhale down for three minutes. Keep your eyes focused on your third eye. Inhale and exhale with your mantra. Breathe with your diaphragm. Do this exercise slowly and gently. For the last three repetitions slow down even more, and don't raise your arms over your head. On the last inhalation just come to a normal standing posture, and hold the breath for about five seconds. Finally, relax the breath, and continue standing while you mentally continue to repeat the mantra. After a minute, sit down and begin your meditation.

Before beginning even this simple yoga exercise program, you should check with your physician, chiropractor, or other health care professional to be sure that the exercises are proper for you. In any case, do these exercises gently. Avoid hard ballistic movements. Your breath, mantra, and concentration—not physical force or speed—are what give yoga its power.

5

🍃 WHAT ELSE? 🍃

Many other practices can help prepare you for meditation. Religious services, silent walking, inspirational reading or music, yoga, traditional tribal music and dancing, and martial arts can all serve in this way. Meditation can stand alone, but I think perhaps it should not. We need more than one or two techniques. We need a way of life. The techniques of meditation will help you. They will calm you and lift you up. But, if meditation remains separate from the rest of your life, a thing apart, then it may not transform you, just as taking a vacation from a stressful job doesn't change the job. Take enough time off from work, and you can neutralize the effects of the stress. But transforming the job itself would take a different approach altogether. What about our lives? Should we take breaks from life with meditation, or should we transform life itself? I think the latter. Meditation can provide refuge, but it can also become an integral part of a larger picture, an aspect of a life transformed, a life which unites body, mind, and soul.

The possibilities have no limits. Here are a few general suggestions. As you read, notice what gets your attention and look further on your own. Read a few books, take some classes, talk with people who have explored these paths before you. Then begin to make some commitment. Boldly strive forward on your new path.

So what else can help you meditate? Look for a group to meditate with. This will give you a whole other level of experience. You will have to search out such groups in your own area. Check the Yellow Pages, or bulletin boards in libraries or natural food stores, and ask around. I have faith that you will find like-minded souls if you put forth some effort.

Consider your diet. Most of us tend to eat too heavy of a diet. Begin to eat more foods that are mostly water such as fruits and vegetables. Reduce animal products such as milk, cheese, and eggs, and eliminate flesh such as meat, fish, and poultry. Health, environmental, and ethical issues dictate these choices, but in terms of our present discussion, a light diet will allow you to become more clear and focused. Chew your food thoroughly. Eat slowly and mindfully.

Begin the practice of mentally carrying your mantra with you wherever you go. To perfect spiritual life, you need to maintain a constant awareness of your higher self. With every breath, be mindful and remember your mantra. At work, at play, conversing with friends, always have a part of you remembering. Keep to your neutrality.

Carry your meditative mind with you throughout your day.

Clear your body of all drugs other than required medicines. Even sugar, caffeine, tobacco, and alcohol create a mental and physical see-saw effect within you. These substances swing you mentally and physically from one state to another and back again, over and over as long as you imbibe. You never achieve equilibrium or balance. You never feel satisfied for long. Eventually, your health suffers. If you live long enough, you may live in pain. All this undermines your effort to meditate and become neutral.

Illegal drugs do even greater violence to your body and mind. Don't even try to meditate if you have taken drugs. If you have been using drugs or alcohol in excess, stop long enough to get straight. Then, tune in, do the breathing exercises on page 82–83, the yoga on pages 84–86, and practice any of the meditations. In the quiet after the meditation ask what you need to do to clean up your life. The natural elation from the meditation will contrast sharply with the drugged state and should begin to convince you that drugs have never taken you to a better state of mind.

Meditate with a purpose. After a meditation, in the stillness that follows, focus your mind on that which you wish to manifest in your life or in the world. Visualize your own health, happiness, or holiness. Imagine yourself sharing, serving, and succeeding. Mentally create a world at peace, a more effective organization, or deeper relationships. Then ask the question: "How may I help to create this goodness?" and listen to the answers.

Most of us can benefit from adding exercise to our daily lives. If you carry around too much body weight, or rarely work up an honest sweat, you will probably feel pretty sluggish in meditation. Contemporary life often doesn't demand much of us physically. So we have to create our own demands with aerobics, workout machines, running, swimming, brisk walking and the like. All exhilarate the mind and the body. If you think being on your feet all day at work takes care of your need for exercise, just ask yourself if you feel great at the end of the day. A "no" means that you ought to consider an exercise program.

Martial arts training is one excellent choice for exercise. Find a teacher who emphasizes the values of avoiding confrontation, and of clarity of mind. Martial arts practice will enhance your meditative practice. The martial arts, when studied with a traditional teacher, become a form of meditation in action. Like yoga teachers, however, many Western martial arts teachers don't have much of an understanding of the deeper aspects of their own art and practice, and thus teach on a superficial, physical level. Shop around for the most spiritually inclined teacher. It doesn't matter exactly what she or he teaches, as much as it matters how she or he teaches and what is emphasized.

6

🍃 A FINAL WORD 🍃

I hope that what I have written in these few pages will get you started on a path that is true for you. Life can have an incredible richness and a joy beyond words. We have all been given, regardless of the circumstances of our lives, an opportunity to live with passion. We can each have a full measure of happiness—that is our birth right. We can each give kindness—that is our blessing. We can each be creative, loving, generous, and forgiving. We can each be supported by others who care for us. We can each be healed. But none of these good things are guaranteed. None are given automatically. Perhaps our only job is to create the conditions in which such pleasures can manifest themselves. We are each fully responsible for the quality of our own lives. Meditation is the most powerful tool available for taking that responsibility.

May these words serve you, and may your spirit guide you.

Sat Nam.